STEM CAREERS
ELECTRICAL ENGINEER

by R.J. Bailey

pogo

Ideas for Parents and Teachers

Pogo Books let children practice reading informational text while introducing them to nonfiction features such as headings, labels, sidebars, maps, and diagrams, as well as a table of contents, glossary, and index.

Carefully leveled text with a strong photo match offers early fluent readers the support they need to succeed.

Before Reading

- "Walk" through the book and point out the various nonfiction features. Ask the student what purpose each feature serves.
- Look at the glossary together. Read and discuss the words.

Read the Book

- Have the child read the book independently.
- Invite him or her to list questions that arise from reading.

After Reading

- Discuss the child's questions. Talk about how he or she might find answers to those questions.
- Prompt the child to think more. Ask: Do you know anyone who works as an electrical engineer? What projects has he or she been involved in? Do you have any interest in this kind of work?

Pogo Books are published by Jump!
5357 Penn Avenue South
Minneapolis, MN 55419
www.jumplibrary.com

Library of Congress Cataloging-in-Publication Data

Names: Bailey, R. J., author.
Title: Electrical engineer / by R.J. Bailey.
Description: Minneapolis, MN: Jump!, Inc., [2017]
Series: STEM careers | Audience: Ages 7-10.
Includes bibliographical references and index.
Identifiers: LCCN 2017011756 (print)
LCCN 2017012808 (ebook)
ISBN 9781624965944 (ebook)
ISBN 9781620317174 (hardcover: alk. paper)
Subjects: LCSH: Electrical engineering–Vocational guidance–Juvenile literature.
Electrical engineers–Juvenile literature.
Classification: LCC TK159 (ebook)
LCC TK159 .B35 2017 (print) | DDC 621.3/023–dc23
LC record available at https://lccn.loc.gov/2017011756

Editor: Jenny Fretland VanVoorst
Book Designer: Molly Ballanger
Photo Researchers: Molly Ballanger & Leah Sanders

Photo Credits: Alamy: Aleksandr Kichigin, 5. Getty: Hero Images, 12-13, 19. iStock: zoranm, 16-17. Shutterstock: a_v_d, cover; Hugo Felix, 1; TADDEUS, 3; Rawpixel.com, 4; Olena Yakobchuk, 6-7; Suwin, 8-9; -Taurus-, 10; Golubovy, 11, 14-15; Patrizio Martorana, 18; YAKOBCHUK VIACHESLAV, 20-21; Jelena Aloskina, 23.

Printed in the United States of America at Corporate Graphics in North Mankato, Minnesota.

TABLE OF CONTENTS

CHAPTER 1

· ·

POWER UP!

What would life look like without **electricity**? There would be no TVs. No computers. No electric lights. No smart phones.

Who helps us power up? Electrical **engineers**! They design machines that use electricity. They know how to use its power to make things work.

These engineers make all kinds of electrical **devices**. These devices can be as small as **microchips**. They can be as large as power stations.

DID YOU KNOW?

Thomas Edison invented the electric light bulb in 1879. He tested thousands of designs before getting it right. Lucky for us he didn't quit!

power plant

Electrical engineers work in many areas. Some work in the power **industry**. They design our **power grid**. Others work in **aerospace**. They design instrument panels for airplanes.

DID YOU KNOW?

Electricity comes from the movement of electrons. Electrons are part of atoms, the smallest form of matter. They have a charge. They are attracted to atoms or electrons with an opposite charge. The movement of these charged particles creates an electric current.

CHAPTER 2

WHAT DO THEY DO?

Electrical engineers follow the **engineering design process**. First, they identify a problem. They ask questions.

They think of ways an electrical device could solve the problem. They draw the device. They plan its **circuits**.

Early designs will often have problems. Engineers need to find them. How? They study their plan. They build a **prototype**. They test it. They fix the problems. Then they test it again. They make it better.

TAKE A LOOK!

• •

Engineers draw pictures of their circuits.
This helps them check their design. This one
shows how a **battery** powers a lamp.

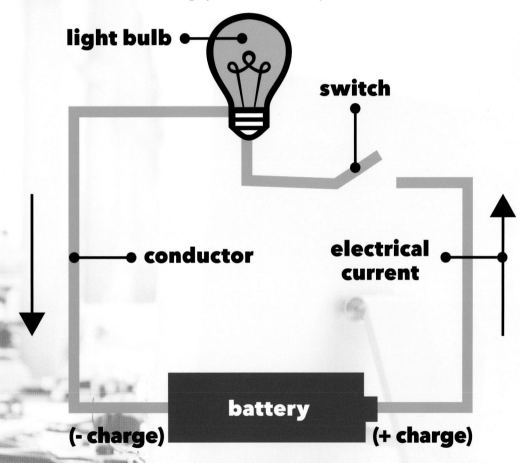

light bulb

switch

conductor

electrical
current

battery

(- charge)

(+ charge)

Electrical engineers often work as part of a team. They direct other engineers and scientists. They make **budgets**, too. They figure the costs of labor and materials.

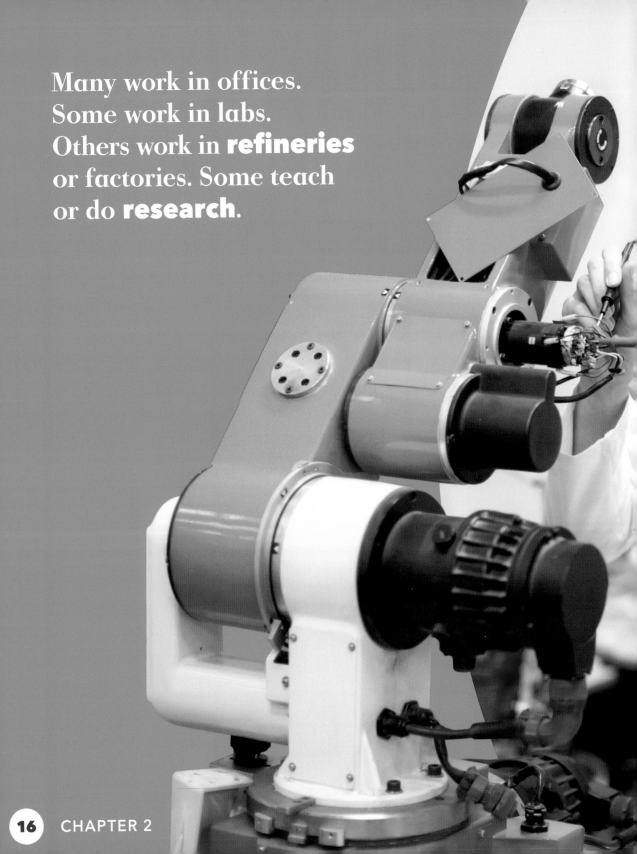

Many work in offices. Some work in labs. Others work in **refineries** or factories. Some teach or do **research**.

CHAPTER 3

BECOMING AN ELECTRICAL ENGINEER

Do you like solving problems?
Do you like making things?
Become an engineer!

What can you do now? Study math. Take computer classes. Do a science project. Later you will need a college degree.

As an electrical engineer, you can shape the future. How? You can make microchips that deliver medicine from inside the body. You can plan the sound system for a sports stadium. You can make parts for robotic aircraft. The possibilities are endless!

DID YOU KNOW?

To work as an engineer, you need STEM skills. What does STEM stand for? Science. Technology. Engineering. Math. STEM careers are in demand. They pay well, too.

ACTIVITIES & TOOLS

TRY THIS!

USING THE EDP

The engineering design process helps us think of ways to solve a problem. For example, let's say you want to make a boat that floats in the bath.

Imagine how you can make it. What materials do you have? You might use cardboard tubes, an empty juice box or plastic bottle, popsicle sticks, tape, glue, construction paper, etc.

Make a plan. Draw a picture of your boat. You may not use all the materials you have gathered. List the ones you plan to use.

Create your boat. Test it in the water. Does it work?

What if it sinks? Improve it. Make changes. For example, use different materials. Return to the earlier steps. Think of different ways to make the boat better.

The engineering design process is a cycle. You can begin at any step. You can move between steps. You can repeat the cycle. And you can use it for almost anything. For example, use it to make a system for keeping your room clean. Your parents will be happy!

GLOSSARY

aerospace: A field that deals with travel in and above Earth's atmosphere.

battery: A container filled with chemicals that produces electrical power.

budgets: Plans for spending a certain amount of money.

circuits: The complete paths that electricity moves along.

devices: Objects, machines, or pieces of equipment that are used for a special purpose.

electricity: A form of energy that is used to run machines and lights.

engineering design process: A chain of steps that engineers follow to solve a problem.

engineers: People who use math and science to solve society's problems and create things that humans use.

industry: A group of businesses that offer a particular product or service.

microchips: Tiny electronic circuits that work together on small pieces of hard material.

power grid: A network for delivering power from suppliers to consumers.

prototype: A first example or model that is used to build the finished product.

refineries: Places where unwanted substances in something are removed.

research: Gathering information or knowledge about something.

INDEX

TO LEARN MORE

Learning more is as easy as 1, 2, 3.

1) Go to www.factsurfer.com

2) Enter "electricalengineer" into the search box.

3) Click the "Surf" button to see a list of websites.

With factsurfer, finding more information is just a click away.